A Crabtree Branches Book

✷ TOP HORSE BREEDS ✷

THOROUGHBRED

Kerri Mazzarella

I0109552

Crabtree Publishing
crabtreebooks.com

School-to-Home Support for Caregivers and Teachers

This high-interest book is designed to motivate striving students with engaging topics while building fluency, vocabulary, and an interest in reading. Here are a few questions and activities to help the reader build upon his or her comprehension skills.

Before Reading:

- *What do I think this book is about?*
- *What do I know about this topic?*
- *What do I want to learn about this topic?*
- *Why am I reading this book?*

During Reading:

- *I wonder why...*
- *I'm curious to know...*
- *How is this like something I already know?*
- *What have I learned so far?*

After Reading:

- *What was the author trying to teach me?*
- *What are some details?*
- *How did the photographs and captions help me understand more?*
- *Read the book again and look for the vocabulary words.*
- *What questions do I still have?*

Extension Activities:

- *What was your favorite part of the book? Write a paragraph on it.*
- *Draw a picture of your favorite thing you learned from the book.*

TABLE OF CONTENTS

HISTORY

The Thoroughbred horse **breed originated** in England in the 1600s. Thoroughbreds are well known for their use in horse racing.

Thoroughbreds are a mix of **native** English and Arabian horses. The Thoroughbred **bloodline** can be traced back to three **stallions** that were brought to England from the Middle East: the Darley Arabian, the Byerly Turk, and the Godolphin Arabian.

The first Thoroughbred to be brought to the United States was a stallion named Bulle Rock. He arrived in 1730.

DID YOU KNOW? The Jockey Club keeps a record of Thoroughbreds in the U.S. and Canada.

The Kentucky Derby is considered America's greatest horse race. Only Thoroughbreds race in the Kentucky Derby. It takes place at the legendary Churchhill Downs racetrack in Louisville, Kentucky.

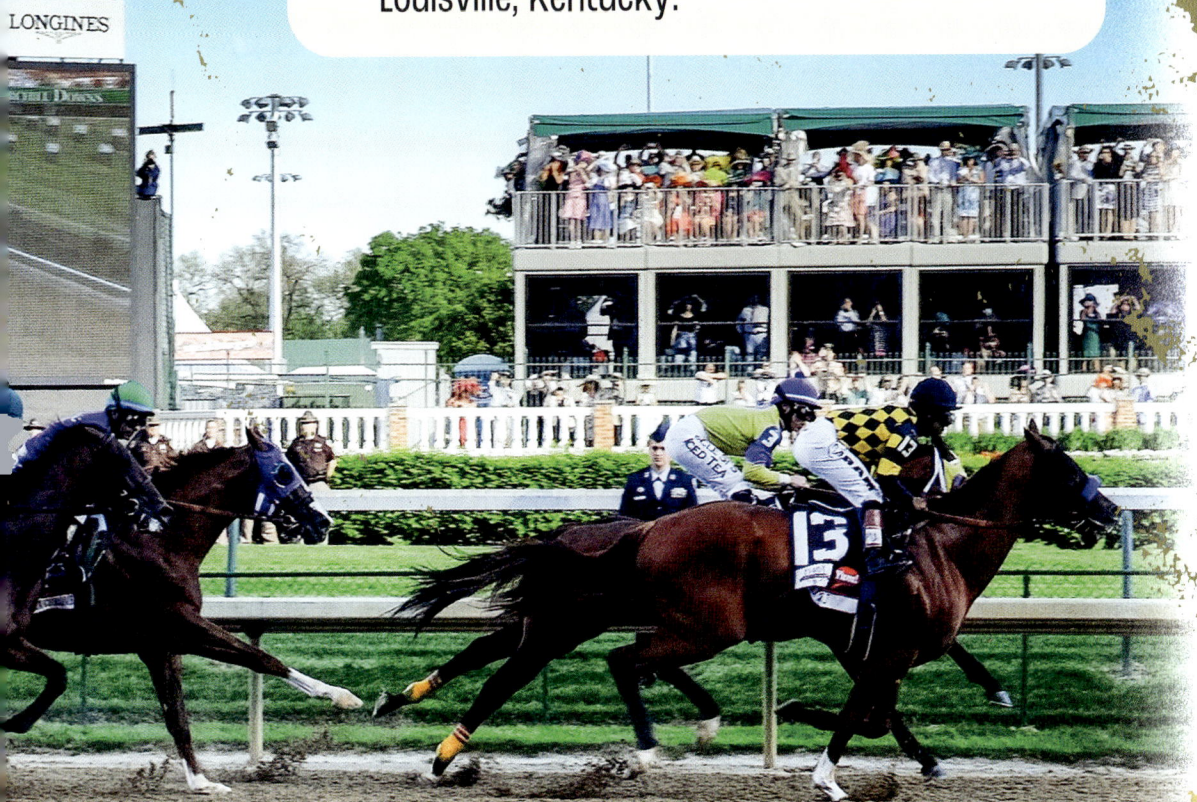

Horse racing became popular in the United States in the 1800s. Tennessee and Kentucky were considered the top locations for breeding and racing horses.

CHARACTERISTICS

Thoroughbred horses have tall, athletic builds. They are one of the fastest racehorses of all time!

Thoroughbreds have strong **hind** legs and a natural ability for jumping. They can run very long distances at very fast speeds.

DID YOU KNOW? Some Thoroughbreds can reach speeds of up to 40 miles per hour (64 km/h).

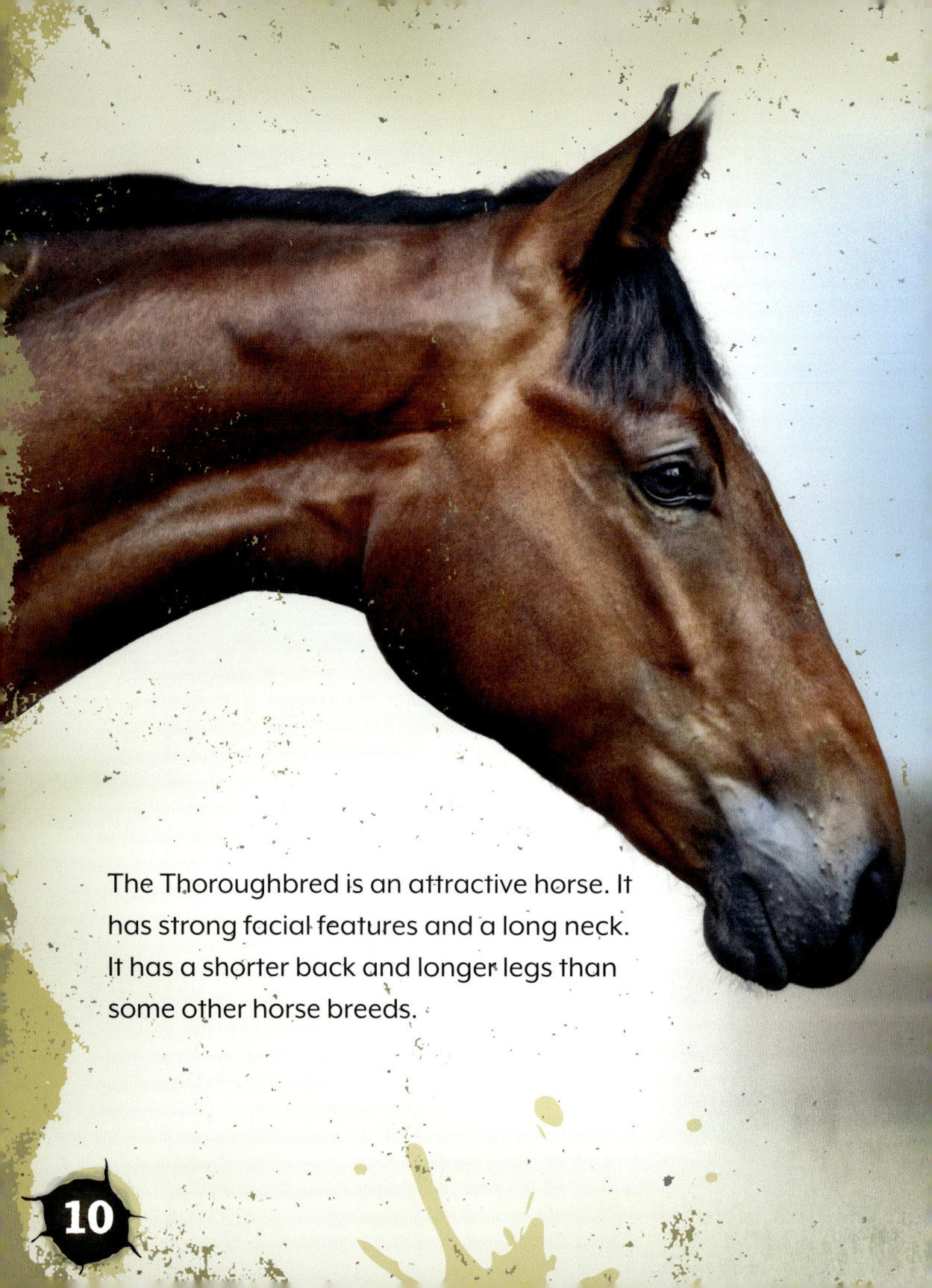

The Thoroughbred is an attractive horse. It has strong facial features and a long neck. It has a shorter back and longer legs than some other horse breeds.

Thoroughbred horses are very intelligent and hardworking. They are part of the **hotblood** group of horses. A Thoroughbred is not the best choice for a beginning rider.

SIZE AND COLOR

Thoroughbreds are considered one of the taller horse breeds. Their height ranges from 15.2 to 17 hands tall.

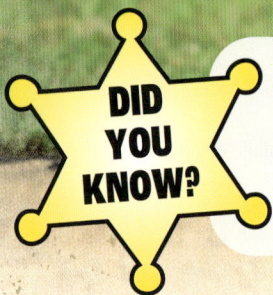

DID YOU KNOW?

A hand is a unit of measurement used to describe the height of a horse. One hand is equal to 4 inches (10.2 cm).

The average Thoroughbred weighs around 1,000 pounds (454 kg). Their lean bodies are built for speed and agility.

Thoroughbreds have short hair with long, thick **manes** and tails. They can be different colors.

DID YOU KNOW? White is the rarest color for a Thoroughbred.

The most common color for a Thoroughbred is bay. Other colors are black, brown, chestnut, roan, gray, and white. They can have white markings on their faces and lower legs.

CARE AND FEEDING

Like all horses, Thoroughbreds require daily exercise and care. Yearly veterinary visits will help them to live a long, healthy life.

DID YOU KNOW?

The average lifespan of a Thoroughbred is 25 to 30 years.

A farrier is a person who takes care of a horse's hooves and horseshoes.

Daily **grooming** is an important responsibility for a horse owner. Bathing and brushing your horse on a regular basis, as well as checking its hooves, are necessary to keep your Thoroughbred happy and healthy.

Thoroughbreds eat a mix of hay, grass, oats, barley, and other grains. A horse that races will have a slightly different diet because they spend more time in their stall and less time **grazing**.

Horses drink a lot of water! It is important to provide 10 to 12 gallons (38 to 45 L) of fresh water each day.

USES, JOBS, AND EQUIPMENT

Thoroughbreds are mostly used in horse racing. They are also used for jumping, **polo**, and fox hunting.

A Thoroughbred that is finished with its racing career is called an off-track Thoroughbred, or OTTB. These horses are great for riding lessons, trail riding, or even therapeutic programs.

A jockey is a person who rides horses in races. They need special equipment for racing horses.

saddle cloth

For all riders, safety should always come first while riding any horse breed. Taking lessons from an experienced trainer is recommended. Be sure to always wear a helmet!

helmet

blinkers

bridle

shadow roll

reins

saddle

jockey

stirrups

bit

girth

COST

The United States breeds more Thoroughbred horses than any other country. The cost of a Thoroughbred racehorse can range from $100,000 to $300,000, depending on the bloodline.

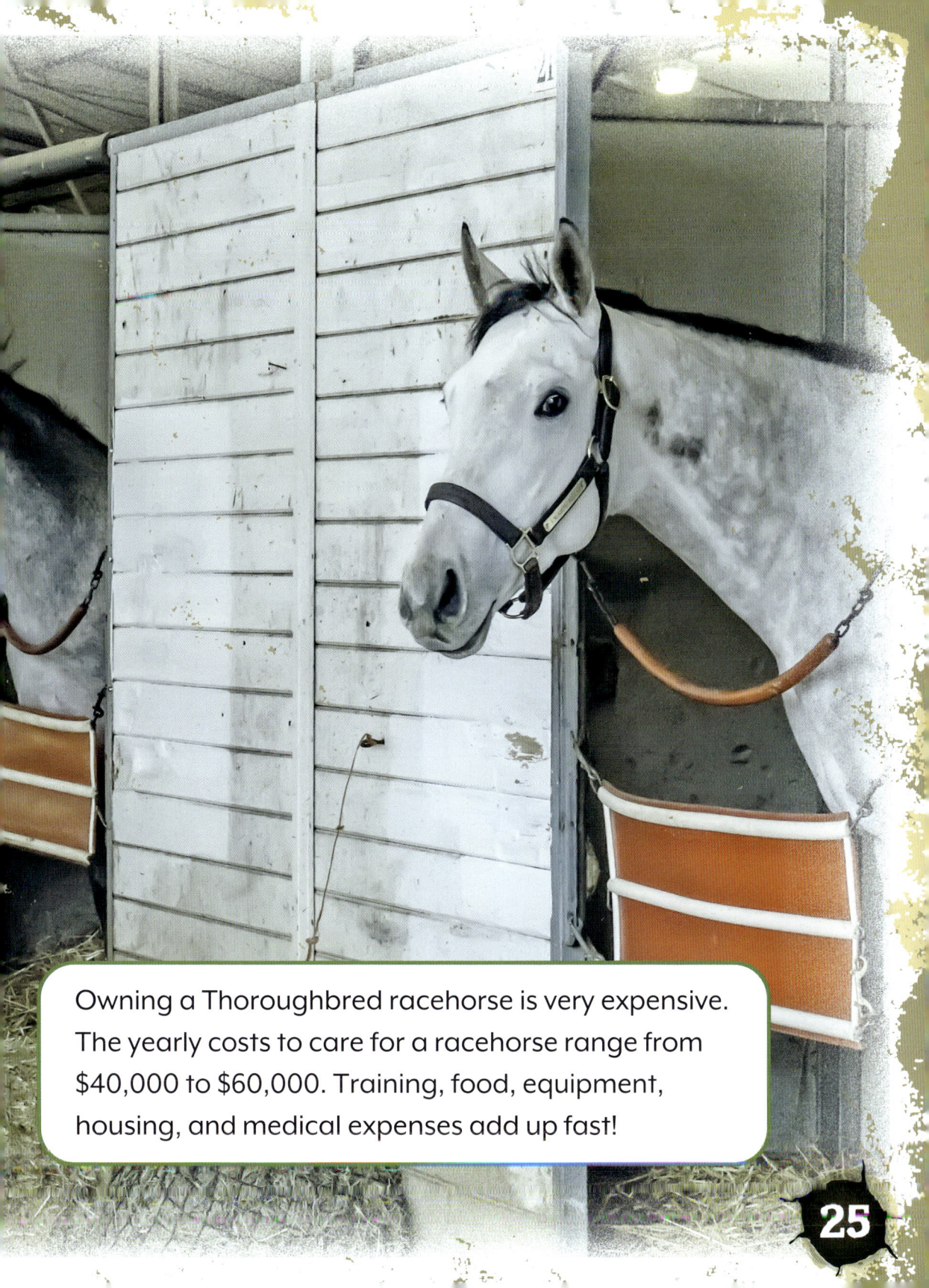

Owning a Thoroughbred racehorse is very expensive. The yearly costs to care for a racehorse range from $40,000 to $60,000. Training, food, equipment, housing, and medical expenses add up fast!

The cost of owning an OTTB is much less. The yearly cost ranges from $4,000 to $10,000.

Housing will be the greatest expense and costs around $6,000 a year on average. Feeding a horse costs around $2,000, and veterinary care costs around $750 each year.

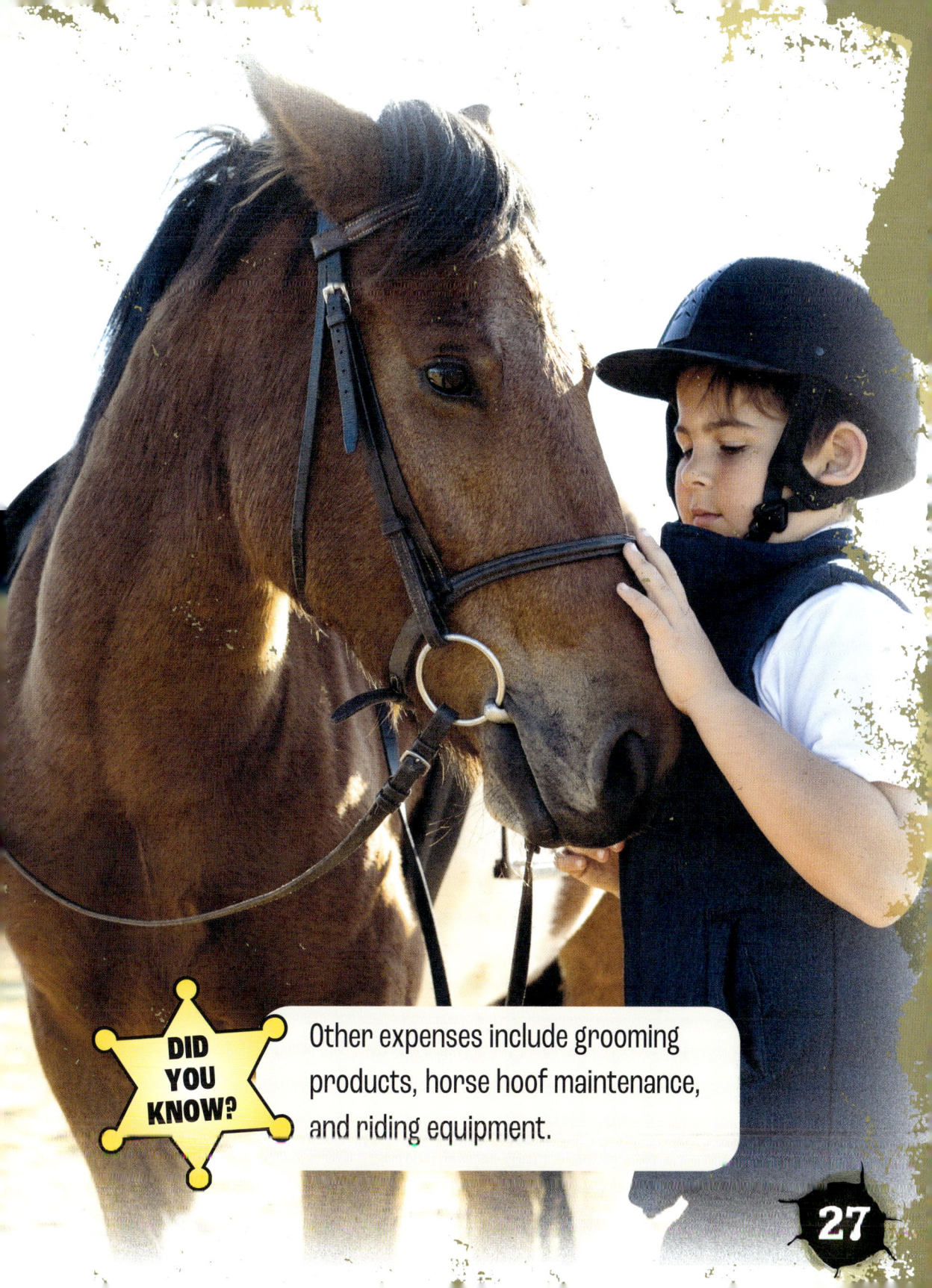

DID YOU KNOW?

Other expenses include grooming products, horse hoof maintenance, and riding equipment.

THE G.O.A.T.s

A Throughbred named Man o' War is regarded as the greatest of all time. During his racing career he won 20 of 21 races. He was **inducted** into the National Museum of Racing and Hall of Fame in 1957.

Secretariat is also considered one of the greatest Thoroughbred horses of all time. He holds the fastest time record for all three races of the Triple Crown. In 2010, a movie called *Secretariat* was made about this amazing racehorse.

The BLOOD-HORSE

A Weekly Magazine Devoted to Improving Thoroughbred Racing and Breeding
Published by the Thoroughbred Owners and Breeders Association

The $1.5-Million Secretariat—More Than Twice The Previous Record

Keeneland Sale Attains Record $67,393 Average

60 CENTS

JULY 26 1976

GLOSSARY

bloodline (BLUHD-lahyn): The ancestors of an animal

breed (BREED): A particular type of animal

grazing (GRAYZ-ing): Feeding on growing grass

grooming (GROOM-ing): The practice of brushing and cleaning the coat of a horse, dog, or other animal

hind (HYND): At the back or rear

hotblood (HOT-blud): A group of athletic horse breeds that are known for their speed and endurance

induct (in-DUHKT): To officially make someone or something a member of a special group

mane (MAYN): The long, thick hair on the head and neck of a horse

native (NAY-tiv): An animal or plant that lives or grows naturally in a certain place

originated (or-IH-jin-ayt-ed): Began to exist or appear

polo (POH-loh): A game played on horseback where players from two teams try to hit a small ball using a long mallet

stallion (STAL-yuhn): An adult male horse

INDEX

WEBSITES TO VISIT

www.thesprucepets.com/meet-the-thoroughbred-1886140

www.britannica.com/animal/Thoroughbred

http://animals.net/thoroughbred/

ABOUT THE AUTHOR

Kerri Mazzarella lives in South Florida with her husband, four children, and two dogs. She loves horses and has always wanted to own one. Her daughter has taken horseback riding lessons for many years. She hopes you enjoy learning about different breeds of horses as much as she does!

Written by: Kerri Mazzarella
Designed by: Kathy Walsh
Series Development: James Earley
Proofreader: Melissa Boyce
Educational Consultant: Marie Lemke M.Ed.

Photographs: Shutterstock Cover & Title pg: Olga_iw, benchart; Background and Border: benchart; p 4: anakondasp; p 5: Jaco Wild; p 6: Bill Brine @ flickr.com; p 8: Jaco Wiid; p 10: Callipso88; p 11: Anaite; p 13: horsemen; p 14: Callipso88, Maria Klubkova; p 16: Aleksandr Rybalko; p 17: Adam Reck; p 18: acceptphoto; p 19: Kartinkin77; p 21: Kento35; p 23: Cheryl Ann Quigley; p 24: Ken Schulze; p 26: Pegasene; p 27: wavebreakmedia; p 28: @Wiki; p 29: emka74

Crabtree Publishing

crabtreebooks.com   800-387-7650
Copyright © 2024 Crabtree Publishing

Printed in the U.S.A./072023/CG20230214

Published in Canada
Crabtree Publishing
616 Welland Ave.
St. Catharines, Ontario
L2M 5V6

Published in the United States
Crabtree Publishing
347 Fifth Ave
Suite 1402-145
New York, NY 10016

Library and Archives Canada Cataloguing in Publication
Available at Library and Archives Canada

Library of Congress Cataloging-in-Publication Data
Available at the Library of Congress

Hardcover: 978-1-0398-0941-3
Paperback: 978-1-0398-0994-9
Ebook (pdf): 978-1-0398-1100-3
Epub: 978-1-0398-1047-1